CONTENTS

PREFACE

The underlying reason for writing this book is our love of skiing. All the people involved in writing the book have skied for many years, mostly since early childhood, and skiing has continued to be one of the most important things in our lives. It's our main winter activity, the reason for the training we do in the weeks before we set off for the slopes, and the source of wonderful memories after each ski season.

Skiing continues to be so appealing to so many people because it offers a superb opportunity for development – who is able to ski as well as they would really like to? And our book has been written to help you reach the next stage of your development in skiing.

Skiing is a combination of fun, physical effort and skill. The fun comes mainly from the excitement of travelling at speed combined with the sense of achievement that comes from managing to keep your balance on an unpredictably slithery, uneven surface. The physical effort of just a week of recreational skiing combined with the pre-ski exercises needed to get the most enjoyment out of it will help to make your body leaner and fitter. And finally, skill ... don't you dream of skiing more elegantly and effortlessly on the

pistes, floating down the powder and confidently finding the best routes through the mogul fields? And that's what our book is all about – finding the unique combination of balance, fitness and skill demanded by this exotic sport.

The pictures we've selected have been included for two reasons. First, to enable you while you're still at home to conjure up the visual pleasure you can get from skiing. The ultra-clear air provides a breathtaking mountain backdrop to the action – where else but at a winter sports resort can you see practically everyone around you dressed in bright colours, moving at high speed as a result of their own efforts and skills? Second, we hope that the photos – especially the multiple-exposure ones – will help you see how you need to move your body to get the best results.

Most books about skiing describe skiing techniques as a set of complex and counter-intuitive activities. But the main point we want to make to you in this book is that as long as you don't get in their way your skis will practically ski themselves and all you need do is cooperate with them. Enjoy yourself!

and

so we begin...

THE THREE ESSENTIALS OF SKIING

A. PHYSICAL FITNESS

How often, waking up on day two of a ski holiday, do you find your muscles are aching so much you can't even get out of bed? Or if you get as far as the ski slope you find yourself stopping every few minutes because your legs just won't support you. The thought crosses your mind: 'Why on earth didn't I get fit for my holiday?' and you make a solemn promise to yourself to do better next time.

Good physical preparation for skiing not only enhances the pleasure of skiing but also makes skiing a lot safer.

Strong legs, and a strong body overall, mean you will have better control of your skis and the route you take, and instead of needing to spend your energy on merely getting where you want to go, you can focus on honing your technique.

Good preparation for skiing isn't difficult and involves neither any special equipment nor a lot of time. All you'll need is a few square metres of floor space and 15 minutes daily, 2–4 times a week for 3–6 weeks (depending on your physical condition to start with and what you're planning to do on your ski holiday) and a bit of ... discipline.

The following pages contain a great range of skiing exercises and examples of training programmes.

THE EXERCISES

>> SQUATTING AGAINST THE WALL

1. Stand against the wall and take up a position as if you were sitting on a chair

2. Ensure your back is flat against the wall

3. Make sure your knees are bent at an angle of slightly less than 90 degrees and that they are aligned to your hips

>> SQUATTING WITH ARMS FORWARD

1 Stand straight and bend your knees at an angle of about 90 degrees

2 Stretch your arms out straight out in front of you. Hold this position

3 Check that your feet are flat on the floor and that your knees point forward

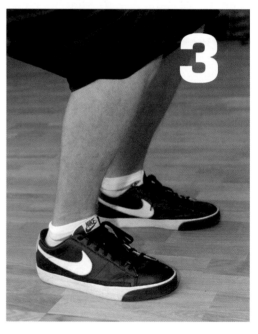

❯❯ SQUATTING, HANDS ON HEAD

1 Stand straight and bend your knees at 90 degrees. Hold this position

2 Put your hands behind your head, making your centre of gravity move slightly backwards

3 Make sure your feet are flat on the floor and that your knees point forward

>> SQUATTING WITH DUMBBELLS

Holding a dumbbell in each hand in the squatting position increases the pressure on your legs.

1 Stand straight, arms by your sides and a dumbbell in each hand

2 Bend your knees at 90 degrees

Inserting a disc under each of your heels increases the tension on the extensor muscles.

1 Stand straight, arms by your sides and place a disc under one heel

2 Place your hands behind your head and bend your knees to about 90 degrees

3 Keep feet flat against the discs

For a slightly more active version of this exercise, bend your knees very slowly extending your arms out straight.

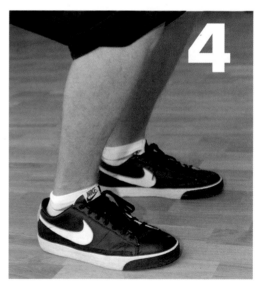

>> ALTERNATING STEP-UPS (5–60 REPETITIONS)

The height of the bench or box you choose should match the length of your lower leg. Place one foot on the step and check that your knee is bent at an angle of no more than 90 degrees with your other foot remaining flat on the floor.

1 Step up with your right foot onto the bench, then your left foot

2 Standing with both feet flat on top of the bench, make sure your weight is distributed evenly on both feet

3 Step down with your right foot, then the other

4 Instead of using a step bench you can use any flat and stable piece of furniture. The higher it is the more difficult the exercise will be

>> SINGLE-LEG STEP-UPS (5–60 REPETITIONS)

1 Step with the right foot up on to the bench, then the left

2 Leaving the right foot on the bench, step down carefully with the left, then lower the right leg to the floor. Repeat with the other legs

>> SINGLE-LEG STEP-UPS, INCOMPLETE (5–45 REPETITIONS)

A more difficult version of the previous exercises; without balancing both feet on top of the bench you will notice more pressure on the muscles.

1 Step up onto the bench with the left foot

2 Lift yourself up using just your left leg. Don't rest your right leg on the bench, but keep it out to one side

3 Step back onto the right foot on the ground, keeping your left foot on the bench, then bring your left foot down. Repeat with the other leg

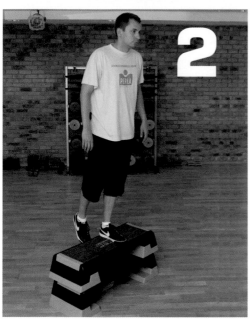

>> ALTERNATING LUNGES (3–35 REPETITIONS)

When performing lunges aim to keep the upper body neutrally aligned and knees vertically aligned to the active foot.

1 Stand in a straight and neutral position, looking forward

2 Step forward with your right leg bent, and bend your back leg

3 Step back to the starting position with your right foot

4 Repeat the lunge with your left leg

>> LUNGES WITH KNEES BENT (3–35 REPETITIONS)

1 Stand with your left knee slightly bent in a half lunge position

2 Step forward with your left foot and bend both legs

3 Make sure your front leg is bent at a 90 degree angle and that your other leg is bent only slightly so that it almost touches the floor

>> LUNGES WITH KNEES BENT WITH DUMBBELLS (2–30 REPETITIONS)

Increasing the load on your upper body will result in a more intense exercise.

1 Stand upright, arms by sides and a dumbbell in each hand

2 Perform the lunges with knees bent exercise (page 23)

>> SINGLE-LEG LUNGES (3–35 REPETITIONS)

1 Stand in a straight and neutral position, looking forward

2 Lunge as shown in exercise on page 22

3 Return to starting position

To increase the effect, use the same foot each time.

>> SINGLE-LEG BACKWARD LUNGES (3–35 REPETITIONS)

1 Start in neutral position, standing straight

2 Take a long step back-ward and bend your knees

3 Move back to the start position

4 Alternate your right and left foot

1 Start in a kneeling position

2 Lean backward; your body should extend in a straight line from your upper legs, but if you find the exercise too difficult at first, bend your body forwards slightly at the hips

3 The degree to which you bend back depends on your ability – the deeper the bend, the more difficult the exercise

>> LEG EXTENSIONS KNEELING ON ONE KNEE (2–30 REPETITIONS)

1 Kneel on your right knee, with both knees bent at 90 degrees

2 Extend the front foot forward on the floor and lift the toes

3 Return the foot to its original position

4 Close-up of toes lifted in extended position

>> RISING ONTO THE TOES, ONE LEG (5–60 REPETITIONS EACH LEG)

1 Stand on your left leg, lightly touching the wall for balance, and rise onto your toes

2 Close-up of toes lifted in extended position

3 Flatten your left foot to return to the starting position

>> RISING ONTO THE TOES, BOTH LEGS (7–90 REPETITIONS)

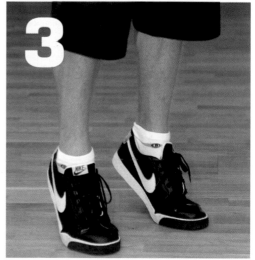

1 Stand on both legs

2 Rise onto your toes

3 Close-up of toes extended

>> RUNNING ON THE SPOT WITH HIGH KNEES (CONTINUE UNTIL TIRED)

1 Stand upright in neutral position

2 & 3 Run on the spot, lifting your knees energetically to at least the height of your hips

4 Close-up of lifting the knees to hip height

>> HEEL FLICKS (CONTINUE UNTIL TIRED)

1 Stand upright in neutral position

2 & 3 Run on the spot, but this time keeping your knees together

4 & 5 Flick your heels up towards your buttocks, touching them if possible

>> KNEE RAISE, CLAP UNDER THE KNEES (CONTINUE UNTIL TIRED)

1 Stand upright in a neutral position

2 Run on the spot, lifting each knee high enough to clap the hands beneath the thigh

3 & 4 The claps ensure you will lift your knees good and high

>> SQUAT THRUST JUMPS (2–25 REPETITIONS)

1 Squat with your hands flat on the floor

2 Jump your legs straight out in a backward thrust

3 Jump back to the starting squat position

4 Jump straight upward so that your body and arms are vertical

5 Land in a squal with your hands in front of you

6 Jump your legs back into the original squatting position again, ready for …

7 The next thrust …

8 And the next jump

>> ALTERNATING LEG SQUAT THRUSTS (2–20 CYCLES, RIGHT AND LEFT)

1 Start as for squat thrusts (page 34)

2 Jump your right leg into an extended position

3 Then switch legs, jumping each time

4 Close-up, one leg extended

5 Close-up, switching legs

>> FROG LEAPS (2–30 REPETITIONS)

1 Start in a squatting position with your hands either side of your neck

2 Rise swiftly, as though you're planning to jump – but keep your knees bent throughout, and keep your feet on the floor

3 Return to the squatting position

4 & 5 Rise swiftly – but this time, jump as high as possible. Return to the squatting position

>> WALKING LUNGES (2–30 REPETITIONS)

1 Walk forward, dropping into a lunge at each step

2 Make sure your body stays upright all the time

3 Keep your front knee, bent at a right angle, over your front foot

Below is a 6-day training programme. By the time you have repeated this 2–3 times in cycles of 2–3 weeks, you will be well prepared for a skiiing holiday. Each workout takes around 30 minutes.

The repetitions suggested for each exercise are just a general guideline and you can vary these according to your physical condition, your age and how much you enjoy the different exercises. The idea is to set yourself a challenge resulting in a certain amount of effort, but not to overdo it. It's important to enjoy what you're doing and get satisfaction out of your progress!

Day	Exercise	Starter programme		Advanced programme	
		Reps in a cycle	Cycles	Reps in a cycle	Cycles
1	alternating lunges	5	1	30	1
	squatting against the wall	until tired	1	until tired	1
	rising onto the toes, both legs	13	1	80	1
	walking lunges	4	1	25	1
	alternating step-ups	8	1	50	1
	running on the spot with high knees	until tired	1	until tired	1
2	single-leg lunges	5	2	30	2
	squatting, hands on head	until tired	1	until tired	1
	rising onto the toes, one leg	8	2	50	2
	frog leaps	4	1	25	1
	single-leg step-ups	8	2	50	2
3	single-leg backward lunges	4	2	25	2
	squatting with arms forward	until tired	1	until tired	1
	kneeling leanbacks	3	1	15	1
	alternating leg squat thrusts	3	1	20	1
	single-leg step-ups, incomplete	7	2	40	2
4	leg extensions kneeling on one knee	4	2	25	2
	squatting with dumbbells (women 2 kg, men 5 kg)	until tired	1	until tired	1
	rising onto the toes, both legs	13	1	80	1
	running on the spot with high knees	until tired	1	until tired	1
	lunges with knees bent	5	2	30	2

5	squatting with disc	until tired	1	until tired	1
	alternating lunges	5	2	30	2
	single-leg backward lunges	4	2	25	2
	alternating leg squat thrusts	3	1	20	1
	lunges with knees bent with dumbbells (women 2 kg, men 5kg)	4	2	25	2
6	slow squatting with arms forward	4	1	25	1
	single-leg lunges	5	2	30	2
	single-leg backward lunges	4	2	25	2
	knee raise, clap under the knees	until tired	1	until tired	1
	squat thrust jumps	3	1	20	1

B. BALANCE

One of the greatest pleasures, but also the challenges, of skiing is generated by what the skier is actually doing – sliding downhill on a slippery slope. Bearing in mind that balancing on moving skis is in itself far more difficult than most other ways we humans have of moving on a rough and uneven surface, it becomes more complicated when you combine this with the movements we need to make on skis – frequent and multi-axis shifting of our centre of gravity from one leg to the other, from one side of a ski to the other, and from tip to tail and vice versa. What it all boils down to is that *skiing involves a continuous rebalancing of our centre of gravity on skis that are moving over terrain that's constantly changing in both direction and texture. It's hard to imagine a tougher challenge to our sense of balance!*

A good skier basically needs to learn the skill of balancing on the move. This skill is not inherent and it needs to be learned well, because in our normal daily lives we hardly ever move in a way that challenges our sense of balance the way skiing does. To improve your sense of balance and prepare properly for a skiing holiday, it's helpful to use something that will imitate the instability of skiing. One such item invaluable for balance is a pair of balance/stability discs (available from shops selling fitness/rehabilitation equipment or online). What follows are basic balance exercises and a training programme that includes ways you can use stability discs.

>> BALANCING ON A ROPE

1 Having laid a rope or belt out on the floor in a straight line, carefully walk along it

2 To make the exercise more challenging, do it with a book on your head

>> SQUATTING ON TWO DISCS

1 Stand upright with each foot on a disc

2 Slowly bend and extend your arms forward

3 Squat down and hold for as long as possible

>> SINGLE LEG-BALANCE ON DISC

Stand on one leg on the balance disc. Maintain this position for as long as possible – if you reach 2 minutes, you have done well!

>> BALANCING ON ONE LEG, BENDING FORWARD

1 Stand on your left leg, then bend your body forward and extend the right leg backward

2 Maintain this position as long as you can – or until you get bored!

>> BALANCING ON ONE LEG, BENDING FORWARD, ON A DISC

Once you find the last exercise easy, repeat it, but this time add in the disc.

1 Place the disc under your left foot and lift your right leg

2 The position from the side

3 Lean forward and hold for as long as you can

>> SINGLE-LEG SQUAT

1 Standing on your right leg, extend the left leg forward

2 Squat down as far as you can, and hold this position

3 & 4 Come back up and repeat

1 Standing on your right leg on a disc, extend the left leg forward

2 Squat down as far as you can and hold this position

3 Repeat with the other leg

4 Repeat with the first leg

>> LUNGING FORWARD ON TWO DISCS

1 Arrange two discs so that they will be beneath your feet when taking a large step forward

2 Stand on the back disc, step forward onto the front one, bend both knees into a semi-squat, and hold. Repeat with the other leg

>> SHIFTING YOUR WEIGHT ON DISCS

1 Stand with your legs apart, each foot on a disc

2 Shift your weight from side to side so that almost your entire weight is taken by one leg

3 Then do the same on the other leg

>> STANDING ON TOES ON DISCS

1 Stand with your legs slightly apart, each foot on a disc

2 Rise onto your toes

3 Place your heels back down onto the disc

4 Rise onto your toes again, and so on

 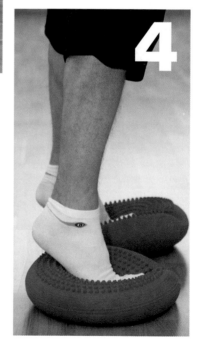

>> SHIFTING WEIGHT FORWARD AND BACKWARD ON DISCS

1 Stand with your legs slightly apart, each foot on a disc, and semi-squat

2 Transfer your weight to your toes, ending with your heels lifted up off the discs

3 Transfer your weight back to your heels, as far as possible

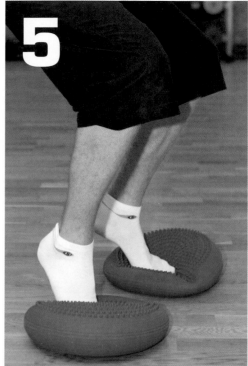

4 Return your weight to your toes, and so on

5 Close-up of heels lifted

>> ARM WRESTLING ON DISCS

1 Stand facing a partner, both of you standing on two discs

2 Clasp right hand to right hand and arm wrestle! Try to stay on the discs

3 Repeat, clasping left hands

⟫ ARM WRESTLING STANDING ON ONE DISC

1 Stand facing your partner, each balancing on your right leg, standing on a disc

2 Clasp right hand to right hand and arm wrestle! Try to stay on the disc

3 Repeat, standing on left legs and clasping left hands

C. TECHNIQUE

Alpine skiing – by which I mean skiing down a series of slopes, and using ski lifts to regain altitude – *is a sport that involves a considerably more complex technique than other types of movement on land, such as running, cycling, skating and cross-country skiing*. And despite the fact that the introduction of carving skis (see page 62) has made the technique easier, mastering the skill still involves a lot of time and effort for most of us.

PERFECT TECHNIQUE

Why should we work on continually improving our skiing technique? There are several good reasons. First, extensive practice – especially with the latest carving skis – lets us reap the full potential offered by the sport and so gain more pleasure and satisfaction from skiing. Second, a better technique gives us better control over our skis, so skiing is much safer for us and for others; we're not going to cause a crash if we can control our speed and direction properly. Third, the better our technique, the less effort we need to make; subtle movements of our upper body and legs and the correct transference of our weight are far more efficient than laboriously heaving our bodies around bends and over bumps. It means that we get less tired and can enjoy ourselves for longer each day. Finally, we can gain a lot of satisfaction simply by virtue of the fact that we're getting better at a challenging sport that we enjoy.

So let's perfect our technique!

NEW STYLE SKIING – CARVING TURNS

Carving skis will ski themselves if you let them!

Every now and then there's an invention or innovation that is held up as being completely revolutionary, a new idea that will totally change both the principles and the way of doing a sport or even a fundamental lifestyle. But although its supporters may be 100 per cent confident that the idea will be widely accepted and put into practice, it is it's users who accept or reject it and, ultimately, cause a revolution or not. The Internet, mobile phones and low-cost airlines are examples of successful lifestyle revolutions. In winter sports the introduction of the free technique in cross-country skiing was a successful revolution, whereas mono-skiing (invented in the 1960s – Alpine skiing on a single broad ski with feet pointing in the direction of travel – you've not heard of it? Hardly surprising!) turned out to be a flop.

The introduction of carving skis has been a highly successful revolution in Alpine skiing, and especially in recreational skiing.

So, what differences have carving skis made to skiing? The relationship between the skier and the ski has totally changed; a ski used to be just a straight length of wood or other material that naturally tended to move forward in a straight line, and which could be turned only when the skier, counterintuitively, made the effort to twist their upper body in the opposite direction to the ski's path of travel. But a carving ski is a user-friendly piece of kit with an inbuilt tendency to turn, allowing a skier to move naturally, with his or her body turning the same way as the skis are going. The skier can adapt much more easily to the natural turning tendency of carving skis, and can quickly learn to control the angle and speed of the turns simply by shifting his or her centre of gravity.

the curve taken naturally by carving skis

This natural turning tendency of carving skis is a result of their 'waist'; as you can see from the photo on the left, each ski is made wider at tip and tail and narrower at the mid-section, under the boot (see page 74). So each edge of the ski forms a curving arc, and when the ski is tilted sideways so that one or the other of the edges is the main point of contact with the snow, the ski – and the skier – can't help but follow the curve of that edge.

make sure you have a steady upper body

There's more to it than that. First, the ski tip is also wider than the tail, so that the curve of the edge from tip to waist is a bit tighter than the curve of the edge from waist to tail. This means that putting pressure onto the front part of the ski will help make the turn sharper (useful when entering a turn or wanting to tighten it up mid-manoeuvre). Conversely, putting pressure onto the tail will make the turn more open (on coming out of the turn or, again mid-manoeuvre, if you find you need to adjust your route).

Second, again because of the ski's waisting, its longitudinal flexing (the way a ski bends when supported only on tips and tails) provides another way for the skier to control the sharpness of turns; the more pressure on the middle of the ski, the sharper the turn, and the less pressure, the gentler the turn.

So the main feature of the carving ski – its waisting – combined with its longitudinal flex provides a fantastic range of options for turn control, ranging from simple and basic to subtle and highly skilled. No wonder carving skis have taken off!

a dynamic short turn

It's worth bearing in mind that these combined features mean that **the actual radius of a turn made by a skier can be far shorter than the sidecut radius specified by the manufacturer of the skis.** (What's this? See chapter 3.)

Waisted skis really enhance the pleasure of skiing. The fun arises partly from the freedom of movement and partly from the turn dynamics; edging on these skis gives the skier an incredible feeling of speed when carving a swift and sure turn.

This is because when a skier is moving forward in a straight line, the sensation of speed is determined by the number of metres covered per second, but in a turn it's the angular speed – the number of degrees turned per second – that impacts upon our senses. The tighter the turn, the more intensely we feel the speed and dynamics of the turn we're making. The way our bodies sense this increased angular momentum while we're making short turns makes us feel as though we're moving fast, even though anyone watching us will see our speed as only moderate, since we're not actually covering many metres per second over the ground.

hips flexed sideways

But you also need to be warned that the changes in skiing technique brought about by carving skis are not always a bed of roses.

The forces acting on a skier using carving skis, arising from the increased angular speed in dynamic turns, are a lot stronger than the forces generated in traditional skiing techniques. Carving skis run as though they're on rails, with minimal slipping, and so the skier's legs have to do the job of counteracting the full strength of the centrifugal force generated in each turn. With the straight skis used in the classical technique, however, that force is much weaker, and also the slipping that formed an integral part of the classical turn dissipates a fair bit of the energy, which does not impact so greatly on the skier's muscles.

This is why in order to do carving skiing you have to be super fit – and even then at the end of a full day of it you're probably going to be very tired. But, in the end, that super fitness is one of the things we strive for as part of the pleasure and satisfaction of the sport.

You'll need to be careful of straining your leg joints, especially your knees – you really don't want to injure your knees, as this can cause you trouble for a long time afterwards. The force generated by the carving combined with the bending of the body at the hips puts pressure onto the lateral part of the knee on the outside of the leg. Plus that outside knee is in an unnatural position during a carving turn, if you bend it excessively into the middle of the turn.

So proper exercises before you hit the slopes, and sideways flexing at the hips more than at the knees when you're carving your turns (more about this in chapter 5), will help you to avoid knee injuries.

03

ALL ABOUT SKIS

When you first see the enormous range of skis in a big shop or rental company you might be forgiven for feeling confused. And the information provided in the specifications may not help you much. For example:

- Size: 146/154/162
- Sidecut: 119-70-100
- Radius: 13 m

Therefore we have organised types of ski into three categories – your experience, your gender and the kind of slopes you like skiing on – which should make it easier for you to make sense of it all and choose the right skis for you.

A. YOUR EXPERIENCE

PROFESSIONAL/COMPETITION

These skis are designed for high speed, and they are narrower and stiffer than most other skis. They handle well on harder pistes, but using them successfully requires a lot of skill.

They include two main ski types:

1 Alpine/downhill – designed for making long carving turns at high speed. The skis run well on their edges both on icy slopes and in deeper snow or crud.
2 Slalom – designed for short, rapid turns. They give good edge control, especially on steep or ice-covered slopes.

INTERMEDIATE/ADVANCED

These are for skiers who may ski on any type of snow, from hard-packed piste to the deepest powder. These skis are broader and more flexible than competition skis, making them suitable for skiing in varying snow conditions and at lower speeds, and their wider tips allow easier turning. These skis do not demand such an expert technique as those in the first group.

BEGINNER

Skis for beginners are very soft and flexible, and so they respond well to the skier's body movements at low speeds. Their shape makes turning really simple, since their wider tips and narrower tails mean that skiers can easily skid them around in the final phase of the turn. If you ski for one or two weekends per season, these are probably the skis for you.

B. YOUR GENDER

MEN'S AND WOMEN'S SKIS

More and more ski models are being made in male and female versions. The women's versions tend to be lighter and more flexible than men's, with bindings normally located a couple of centimetres or so further forward, making the skis more stable and facilitating turns. Women do, of course, ski on all types of skis, but those who have the female body type with a centre of gravity lower than that of a typical man, and who tend to rely more on balance and skill rather than on weight and strength, are likely to find women's designs a lot more satisfactory.

C. THE TYPE OF SKIING YOU'LL BE DOING

Racing is outside the scope of this book; here we describe skis for different types of recreational skiing.

ALL-MOUNTAIN/CARVING

All-mountain will be the right skis for the vast majority of recreational skiers, from beginner through to advanced, who ski mainly on pistes. Carving skis are specifically designed for making turns more easily.

FREERIDE/ALL-TERRAIN

These terms describe roughly the same thing – skis that can handle a wide range of terrain and varying types of snow. One of the latest designs to cater for this wide range of purposes is called mid-fat, which are wider than skis designed specifically for pistes, but slimmer than full-scale off-piste skis. The tip width of mid-fat falls within the range

of 100–109 mm, and the width under the boot is over 70 mm – they are wide enough to run fairly well in powder or crud, but not so wide as to make them difficult to control on piste.

OFF PISTE

Fat skis are super wide, enabling them to float on the powder like waterskis. Their tips are normally 110 mm wide or more, with a tail width starting at 100 mm, and they are wide under the boot, too. These skis are fantastic in powder – but in other snow conditions, groomed pistes especially, they can be tricky even for experts to handle.

FREESTYLE

These skis are designed for jumps and tricks in snow parks, alongside snowboarders. They are also used in mogul fields (where most turns are made in the air) and for doing aerobatics. Freestyle skis have hardly any sidecut and upward-curved tails, like their tips, so you can land on them more easily after a jump, or even ski backwards. At only 120–180 cm long, they are shorter than other skis, making them much easier to manoeuvre.

D. SPECIFIC FEATURES OF SKIS

Now we're going to look at the more technical features of skis.

WIDTH OF WAIST

The waist is a relatively short section of the overall length of a ski, but it accounts for its major characteristics. This crucial section is the part under the boot plus about 10 cm in front of and behind it. *The width of the ski in this section determines the ease of rotating the ski onto its edge, and also how deeply that edge will cut into the surface.* The narrower the ski under the boot, the easier it is to edge, so the ski will grip better on hard, icy slopes. However, a narrow ski handles badly on a soft surface, as it sinks deeply into the snow and so is more difficult to turn; in addition the boot protruding on either side of the ski can get caught in the soft snow that's often found at the end of a day.

That is why you need to pay attention to the ski width at the waist – the middle number of the three shown in the sidecut spec (see page 70) – to select the right skis for the type of skiing you plan to do. Skis for carving turns on hard prepared pistes are the narrowest under the boot; their width at the waist is often no more than 68 mm. All-mountain skis start at 70 mm under the boot, and skis designed specifically for off piste are at least 90 mm wide under the boot.

WIDTH OF TIPS AND TAILS

The width of skis at their tips and tails combined with their waist width and their overall length impacts primarily on the ski radius (see below), which has a bearing on what they're used for. Carving and all-mountain skis have tips approximately 120 mm wide and tails around 100 mm wide. Off-piste skis are wider – their tips and tails can be 160 mm and 148 mm wide respectively. At the other end of the spectrum are free-ride skis, with tips and tails about 110–115 mm wide, and these are relatively straight along the length of their edges.

RADIUS

The ski radius – sometimes shown in the spec with just an 'R' before it – tells you what you can do best on specific skis: make a series of short turns, or bomb straight downhill, or something in between.

Because the curve of the edge changes its shape as it goes along the ski from front to back, the calculations used by manufacturers to arrive at the radius figure are hugely complex. Essentially the radius figure is derived from the effective length of the ski (i.e. the length normally in contact with the snow, around 85–90 per cent of the total length) combined with its sidecut, i.e. the difference between width at the waist and the average of tip width added to tail width. A longer effective length and/or smaller sidecut generates a longer sidecut radius; a shorter length and/or bigger sidecut generates a shorter radius.

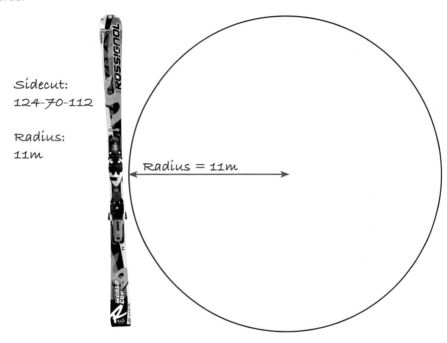

Sidecut:
124-70-112

Radius:
11m

Radius = 11m

So the 'sidecut ski radius', to give it its full title, is the radius of the circle that arises from the average curve of the arc created by the edge of a ski laid flat on the ground.

Don't confuse the sidecut radius with the 'turn radius'. This is a variable number which derives from the sidecut radius but is affected by the weight and the technique of the skier, who can tighten or open up a turn by shifting their weight onto the front or rear of the ski to utilise the varying degree of curve along its length, and can also use the ski's longitudinal flex to edge its centre section more or less deeply, again tightening up or opening up a turn. So a turn radius can be a lot longer or shorter than the sidecut radius specified by the manufacturer.

Now for the numbers: if you want skis designed for fast skiing with long turns on prepared pistes, e.g. racing, downhill, go for models with a longer sidecut radius (20+ m); giant slalom skis are required to have a minimum radius of 21 m. Off-piste and mogul skis have a similar radius.

For all-mountain skis and freeride skis, pick a slightly shorter radius (around 18 m). Working downwards, a radius of around 15 m is good for serious on-piste carving, and slalom skis have a radius of around 13 m. Children's skis will of course have a still shorter radius, perhaps around 11 m.

CONSTRUCTION

The current technologies used in the construction of skis are even more complex than their form. *The era of skis carved from a single length of timber is long gone, and now the construction of skis involves a combination of sophisticated materials and complex manufacturing processes.*

While there is no space here to analyse ski construction in detail, a broad understanding of their structure can be helpful when choosing your skis. The technology is developing rapidly, but there are currently three main divisions into which ski construction falls: sandwich, torsion box and monocoque.

Most skis are constructed as a sandwich in which they are built up in layers, usually with a laminate of something like glass fibre below a central core (see below), and another layer of laminate above it. A torsion box is more sophisticated (hence more expensive), and in its construction the top and bottom layers extend right around the sides of the ski and meet one another to become a single unit that fully encloses the core. Finally, the ultimate, monocoque, is a development of the torsion box in that the core is fully enclosed by the exterior but, in addition, that exterior – which may be made of graphite, metal, glass fibre, or a combination of any of these – is integrally important to the structure of the ski.

Core

The core of the ski has an effect on its weight and to some extent its flex. Current ski construction techniques see the core being made mainly of either wood or various types of synthetic foam. Wood tends to be more durable and responds more directly to the skier's body movements, but is normally more expensive. A foam core is lighter and cheaper, but experts claim that it responds slowly to weight shifting and the skier's movements. Metal added to the core construction increases the weight and stiffens the ski.

Soles

The soles of skis are normally made of polyethylene at present, although in higher quality models they can be made of graphite. Soles produced with less sophisticated technologies can handle badly in extreme temperatures, but they are easier to look after, and minor damage to them is easier to repair.

LONGITUDINAL FLEX

This is what is being referred to when you see 'soft' or 'stiff' in a description of skis. The longitudinal flexibility of skis has a significant influence on where and how they are best used. Stiffer skis are designed for fast skiing on hard prepared pistes. They are more difficult to manoeuvre, and turns on them need to be carried out assertively and precisely.

Softer skis are ideal for beginners due to the ease of turning them and the way they forgive a less-than-perfect technique. Skis for powder are softer, too. All-mountain skis are somewhere in the middle of the stiffness scale.

E. SELECTING YOUR SKIS

How can you find the skis that are best for you at the stage you're at? If you're in doubt, bear in mind that you'll be wanting your investment to last you for some time, so choose a grade up rather than down, to cater for your progress; you can reasonably expect a pair of skis to last for around 100 hours of skiing.

It's best to take advantage of professional advice in a shop or rental company. But *if you need to choose a pair of skis on your own, the two main factors to take into account are your skiing level and style (to select the type and shape of your skis), and your height/ weight (to select their length).*

1 YOUR SKIING LEVEL
Beginner
You are about to start skiing, or you have been skiing for a while but are happier with gentler descents on well-prepared green and blue routes.

You need skis which are easy to control and feel stable, and that turn easily and grip well in a moderately demanding terrain. You would do best to choose *softer skis from the range of recreational all-mountain, or – if you particularly like zigzagging back and forth across the pistes – carving skis.*

Intermediate
You have skied through a few seasons, working on your own technique or learning from an instructor. You can control your speed reasonably well, and you feel confident on red routes and easier black routes. You might like to start developing your skills on steep slopes and moguls, and off piste.

You need skis which respond well to your instructions, with edges that bite well but are still forgiving of a less-than-perfect technique. *Select from the range of intermediate skis, either all-mountain, carving or off-piste.*

Expert
You love the fall line, and move confidently, fast and assertively. You like tackling steep pistes at high speed and/or floating through untouched powder. You need high-quality skis with an excellent response. At this level, *you really should have two or three pairs of skis, each type suitable for specific snow conditions combined with your skiing style.*

2 LENGTH OF SKIS

The guidelines for the length of your skis are mostly very general, but can still be useful, even though they tend to change with the development of skiing techniques – *the development of carving, for example, resulted in skis being made shorter than before.* Basically, the shorter the skis, the easier it is to turn them, but shorter skis are less stable at higher speeds and on hard surfaces; longer skis are more difficult to turn, but are more stable at speed and in tricky conditions.

If you have a fairly average BMI (body mass index), your ski length (the 'size' figure in a specification, usually shown in millimetres) can be related to your height. The current rule of thumb is that expert skiers select skis that reach their forehead, intermediate skiers a pair that reach the tip of their nose, and beginners those that reach their chin.

If you are either more slender than average or overweight you would do better, however, to disregard your height and instead select the length of your skis relative to your weight, as follows:

Weight (kg)	Ski length (cm)
50–56	145
57–62	150
63–67	155
68–74	160
75–81	165
82+	170

At the outset, choosing skis can seem a dauntingly complex process, but the huge range available gives you every chance of finding a pair that's perfect for you. It's just a matter of a bit of basic knowledge – which we've given you – and time ... and of course what you're prepared to spend. A good rule of thumb here is that if you're trying to decide between two models – whether of skis, or cars, or music systems, or anything else for that matter – that are on sale at approximately the same price, it's normally wiser to pick an entry-level model from a high-quality manufacturer than a top-of-the-range one from a budget manufacturer. Over to you!

04

moving
onwards ...

THE ANATOMY OF A TURN

Turning well is what skiing for pleasure is all about. You'll probably come across the occasional speed demon schussing (straight running) down any hill anywhere, but most of us like making a series of linked turns down the hill as in a slalom or a giant slalom. *It's the balance and coordination needed for the turns – the smooth shifting of our weight from one side to the other, and slowing between turns then accelerating in the turns themselves – that makes skiing such fun; a lot more is required of us than straight physical effort.*

Turning allows us to control our speed, to accelerate where conditions permit and slow down if we see a difficult section appearing or we just want to take things a bit easier.

The current fashion for shorter skis that are more deeply waisted, with a smaller turn radius, encourages us – even forces us to some extent – to make turns. The extreme models will actually prevent you from running straight. If you want to find out about this the hard way, try schussing on a pair of slalom skis!

The true essence of skiing is making a series of linked turns.

The trouble is that it's not that easy: *a turn is a relatively difficult manoeuvre, requiring coordination of the upper and lower body, finely tuned balance and skill in steering your skis.* In addition, the type of snow, the steepness of the slope, the weather conditions and the type of skis we use all have their effect on the kind of turn we make. A turn on off-piste skis made in fresh snow on a moderately steep slope will be totally different from a turn on slalom skis made on a steep, hard piste recently laid down by snow cats. Even with the same pair of skis, we are going to turn in a different way depending on the type of slope and the time of day, ranging from sliding around in smooth, generous curves on a freshly groomed red slope in the morning to short, sharp chops and changes in mogul fields, especially in the slight thaw that so often comes at the end of the day. But to counteract that, there are now carving skis, which have almost completely supplanted classical downhill skis. *Carving skis are an absolute gift to skiers, because if you will only let them do it, they'll just turn themselves.*

What you need to learn to do is coordinate the movements of your body and transfer your weight in a way that lets your skis turn in the direction you want them to go in.

A. TYPES OF TURN

Before starting on a detailed analysis of ski turns, let's look at the differences in the types of turns we make on a slope, and the elements that are common to all turns.

LONG TURNS

First, there's the carving turn, a long, wide turn made on edged skis, following the curve of their edges.

Skis cut a curve whose size relates to their waisting and sidecut radius.

This means that slalom skis with a radius specified at 12 m will cut 12-m arcs into the snow, and if the transition phase – traversing the slope – follows straight after finishing each complete turn, and you then go directly into a new turn, your course down the hill should be contained within a corridor 24 m wide. It is a theoretical situation, and it never actually happens – because edged skis when additionally flexed tighten the turn radius, and the transition phase actually starts at the moment when you are still running down the fall line. So your skiing corridor is significantly narrower than the theoretical 24 m. *The clear ski track left on the snow confirms that a turn is made only on edged skis.*

track made by a long turn

This type of turn will be referred to here as a long turn, in order to avoid the ambiguity that could be generated by calling it a carving turn; in fact, every single turn made on waisted skis should be done completely, or at least in part, on edged skis, which means it is in fact a carving turn. When we look back at the track left by any of our turns we will always see deeper or shallower, shorter or longer, grooves clearly showing that we have carved something.

In a long turn, your skis will steer themselves, and you should just leave them to it. The only effort your body needs to make is to maintain the correct, relatively immobile stance; you need to make only a few active movements with your lower body and legs, the upper body, arms and poles remaining almost still.

What you should focus on in a turn – and what plays a key role in all turns – is dynamic balancing and the correct shifting of your weight (i.e. your centre of gravity). *Throughout the turn you should support almost your entire weight on one leg – the outside one.*

weight transferred onto the
other ski, change of edge and
transition into the next turn

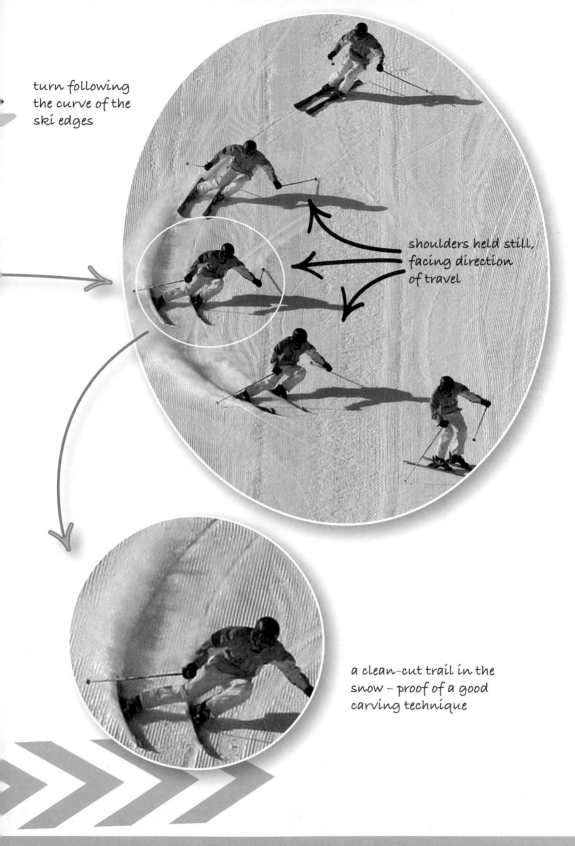

turn following
the curve of the
ski edges

shoulders held still,
facing direction
of travel

a clean-cut trail in the
snow – proof of a good
carving technique

THE BASICS

at mid-turn

turn radius

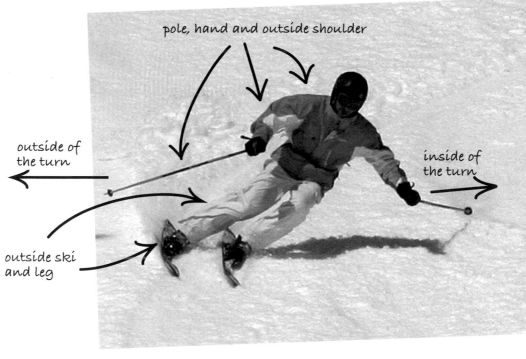

pole, hand and outside shoulder

outside of
the turn

inside of
the turn

outside ski
and leg

a long turn

You need to keep a balanced position fore and aft with a little weight on the ski tips, especially at the start of the turn.

In the transition between turns you need to seamlessly take the weight off what was the outside ski and transfer your weight onto the other ski, which will then become the outside ski in the next turn.

A well executed, smooth long turn gives a great feeling of satisfaction to the skier, and it looks good, too.

SHORT TURNS

The short turn falls at the other end of the turning spectrum. The skis run on their edges for most of this turn, edged and flexed to the maximum, but *if the slope is narrow, steep or crowded, you may have to make a tighter turn than dictated by the skis' geometry, and so this turn may well involve a small degree of skidding.*

Your movements are much more active overall than in the long turn; the upper body gets involved in the action, and you should use your poles to mark the rhythm of your turns, even going so far as to plant each one as an axis around which the turn is made.

the ski track in a short turn

TIGHTER TURNS

the ski turn radius is shorter than the manufacturer's specification →

legs hip-width apart

the pole marks the apex of the turn

quick turns force the body to be directed a bit down the slope

dynamic short turn

The way we balance and shift our weight in a short turn is similar to what we would do in a long turn, but our movements are faster and stronger; short turns are very satisfying to do and great fun to watch.

Between these extremes there are other types of turn, referred to collectively as mid-radius turns.

B. PHASES OF THE TURN

Just as with classifying turns themselves, to try and divide the continuous evolution of a turn into separate sections is a somewhat artificial exercise. However, to make it easier for you to learn the various elements involved in making a turn, we have divided it into several phases that follow opposite.

2 turn completion

1 turn correctly

3 transition

4 turn initiation and control

We'll start at the phase which is not actually part of a turn, but links them – the transition; this is the interval between the end of one turn and the start of the next. *The transition phase can take place so fast it's almost impossible to detect it, or it can take some time.* If you see a photo of a skier in the transition phase it can be difficult to work out which way they have turned last and which way they'll be going next.

3 transition

centre of gravity over the skis

skis lying flat on the snow

This is because in the transition phase both skis are running flat on the snow, the skier's weight is equally distributed in both the fore-and-aft axis and the right-and-left axis, and the arms and poles are level with one another. The overall stance of the skier can be either bent (in the compensation technique) or visibly upright (in the down-and-up technique). In order to make a smooth turn you can employ two different techniques – both of which lifts weight off the skis (unweighting). The compensation technique consists of maintaining a steady upper body and changing your weight from ski to ski quickly. The down-and-up technique is employed by going down slowly then jumping the backs of the skis up. As they unweight, you can get them round. This down-and-up motion works the legs, and is also an elegant way of turning.

In this phase, because skis are unweighted, they can also be easily rotated, especially on very steep slopes. This is a useful racing technique.

transition in the
compensation
technique

3 transition

transition in the down-and-
up technique

jumping in the transition phase

skis off the ground at the momen
when the centre of gravity moves
from one side to the other

The transition phase, as the name implies, leads the skier on to the next phase, **turn initiation**. All the elements which in transition were in balance and in a neutral state now become active, dynamic and clearly visible.

First of all, **the skier's centre of gravity shifts towards the axis of the next turn, the skier's body clearly leaning in that direction.** At the same time the skier's stance may either become more upright (in the compensation technique) or remain extended (in the down-and-up technique).

The skier's weight, which had been equally balanced between the skis in the transition phase, is now put onto the outside ski, and pressure is put onto the tips of the skis; the icier the conditions, the more pressure needs to be put onto the front of the skis at this phase of the turn. The skis are visibly edged. If the turn is to be a long one, the arms should remain still, or to initiate a short turn the inside arm should swing forward ready to plant a pole.

4 turn initiation

centre of gravity clearly
over the inside of the turn

weight mainly on
outer ski

turning correctly

These movements of the turn initiation phase develop into the **control phase**. The skier starts to lean over so that their body is shifted to a position vertically above the ski on the inside of the turn; photos taken of a skier in the transitional or initiation phase are not impressive, but photos taken in this phase are far more dynamic and interesting.

The fore-and-aft centre of gravity is located more or less over the midbody of the skis, though with a slight pressure on the tips of the skis. In a dynamic turn, the skis are deeply edged and relatively wide apart but due to the way the body is slanting, the legs are close together and sometimes the knee of the outside leg will almost touch the boot of the inside leg. Even though the centre of gravity is above the inside ski, on a steep piste and in a faster turn it is in fact the outside ski (and leg) that takes almost the entire weight, but on more gentle slopes, at lower speeds and in softer snow the body is more upright and the weight is more evenly distributed between the skis.

It's the control phase that generates so much of the pleasure of skiing: the dynamics of the turn and our deeply edged skis give us the euphoric sensation of speed, and we know we're looking good!

But all good things come to an end and every turn develops unavoidably into the next phase – *turn completion*.

bending the hips deeply

knees bent moderately

2 turn completion

leaning towards the
centre of the turn

leaning the body and bending through
the hips and knees force the
skis to be firmly edged

Just as going into the turn involved making stronger and more asymmetric movements, the completion phase features the opposite; the weight begins to shift from the inside of the turn to become more evenly balanced over both skis, and the sideways slant of the body is reduced as we stand more upright.

bending the knees
and turning

the turn completion
phase

leaning to the side
decreases

In the fore-and-aft axis, our centre of gravity moves back to either come over the midbody of the skis or be shifted slightly backward. The skis are still visibly edged, but less than at the apex of the turn, and their flex is reduced. We are still putting a fair bit of pressure onto the outside ski, but now we're adding weight onto the inside ski as well. In a long turn, the upper body and poles remain almost still, and in short turns we will already be thinking about planting the pole for the next turn.

Completion leads to transition and on to the next turn, the whole procedure to be repeated in the opposite direction.

the centre of gravity may shift

down and up

transition

compensation

turning correctly

turn initiation

turn completion

C. ELEMENTS OF THE TURN

BODY WEIGHT

Skiing is like playing a game with our balance and the dynamic shifting of our centre of gravity. Without going into the deep theory of it, I'd like to stress that the various forces that act on us in skiing – a highly dynamic sport – differ fundamentally from the forces acting on our body when we're standing still. Then, it is just gravity that acts vertically downward on our body, and gravity is the only factor that determines the location of the centre of gravity of our body in relation to our feet – but the dynamics of skiing create a situation that is far more complex.

In ski turns, centrifugal force also needs to be taken into account. Depending on how dynamically we turn – that is, how fast we're moving over the ground and how tightly or gently we're turning – *centrifugal force impacts significantly on our centre of gravity, and may even be the overriding factor that determines its location.*

The situation becomes even more challenging when we acknowledge that when we're standing still we're interacting with gravity through the soles of our feet, a relatively wide and steady base; but when we're skiing the interaction often takes place through the very narrow, and hence, unstable line generated by the edges of skis that, being in motion, are themselves unstable as a whole. So the task is very difficult: when we're skiing, due to the dynamically changing forces and the lie of the land, the base we're depending on is doubly unstable. In this situation we need to make full use of our sense of balance and our muscles. The challenge is tough, exciting and at times even dangerous, but then our satisfaction when we pull it off successfully is tremendous.

The laws of physics tell us that any moving object tends to continue in a straight line – this is called 'momentum'. If we make our skis turn, that momentum, which when we're turning we perceive as centrifugal force, would result in our body carrying straight on in the same direction as before and falling because our feet have changed direction and are no longer beneath us. So, what happens to our centre of gravity when we're skiing? We must use it to counteract the centrifugal force.

To do this we need to lean towards the inside of the turn, making the line running between our centre of gravity and the point of contact of our skis with the ground align with the combination of gravity and centrifugal force. We have to rely on the strength of our bones and muscles to balance this equation.

The diagonal slant of our body depends primarily on our speed and to a lesser extent on the type of the turn. The deeper, faster and tighter we turn, the more acute the slant must be: it ranges from a gentle lean in slow, long turns to almost horizontal in fast, short, slalom-style turns.

the amount of lean depends mainly on speed, but also on the turn radius

moderate lean in a fairly short turn

leaning well over in a short but very dynamic turn

The same rule applies in the individual turn phases. The transition phase is the time when we are not turning and we are going straight. No centrifugal force is acting on us, and our bones and muscles need to counteract only the force of gravity; as when we're standing still, our centre of gravity is vertically over the centre of the area marked out by our skis.

turn initiation – low speed – slight lean

centrifugal force

gravity

resulting force

When we start making a turn, our angular speed is relatively low and we're following a wide arc. Centrifugal force is therefore low and we need to be leaning over only a little.

the degree of lean depends on our speed and the phase of the turn

But as we go into the control phase, we put pressure onto the ski tips and so tighten the turn radius; as a result of the law of conservation of momentum we accelerate. So **centrifugal force increases rapidly, pulling us outwards, and in response to that we must, if we want to stay on our feet, lean our body further over**, shifting our centre of gravity towards the inside of the turn so that it is directly above the snow rather than over our feet.

turning correctly – high speed – leaning well over

centrifugal force

gravity

resulting force

distribution of forces and location of the centre of gravity in the control phase

To come out of a turn, we reduce the pressure on our skis and so reduce their degree of flex; we also shift our weight slightly backward to bring the shallower curve of the ski tail edge into play. These two actions result in an increase in the turn radius and again there will be a response to the law of conservation of momentum, this time slowing down. *The combination of slower speed and greater turn radius result in the centrifugal force decreasing, and this in turn allows us to lean sideways less and reduce the shift in our centre of gravity, bringing it back over our feet again.*

So the game we're playing with our centre of gravity consists of shifting it smoothly from an extreme diagonal lean at the apex of one turn through a very temporary position directly over our skis in the transition phase, and then going to the next extreme by leaning in on the next turn. On the surface this looks simple, but in fact, given the tremendous forces acting on us and the narrow base of the ski edges on which we're balancing, it's something like balancing on a tightrope while carrying a sack of potatoes. The margin for error is similar, too, in that an angle of lean that's insufficient or too deep can make us fall – but luckily this is going to be on terrain that's relatively friendly.

Once again we stress – an acute sense of balance is one of the three basic attributes of a good skier.

PATHS TRAVELLED BY THE SKIS AND THE SKIER

The regular shifting of the skier's centre of gravity from one side to the other makes the skier's centre of gravity travel along a different path than that traced out by the skis. The skis move along a path linking alternating arcs, wider or narrower, depending on the type of turn.

Both the skier's body and their skis swing down the hill together, but the skis should be leaving behind them a track on the ground that's significantly wider than the route taken by the skier's body. In a championship slalom, the competitors' shoulders can travel in an almost straight line down the hill above skis that swing out in short, sharp arcs from side to side beneath them.

the tracks left by skis, in a wide turn (above) and narrow turns (below)

the lines followed by the skier's centre of gravity

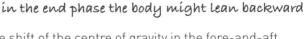

in the end phase the body might lean backward

The shift of the centre of gravity in the fore-and-aft axis is much less obvious, perhaps even imperceptible.

In the transition phase, you should be perfectly balanced, positioned directly above the centre of your skis in both directions: right and left, and fore and aft. To initiate the turn, shift your weight slightly forward – you can sense this by feeling the increased pressure on your shins from the tongues of your boots – and you will then be engaging the front, and more deeply curved, section of the ski edges to tighten the turn radius. In the control phase, if you want to tighten the turn to a sharper one than the sidecut radius normally gives you, you will need to continue leaning forward slightly, or if you want to take advantage of the natural arc of the whole ski, you should return your weight to the midbody.

in balance, in transition

In the completion phase, shift your weight slightly backwards, engaging the rear, less waisted part of the skis; this will reduce the turn radius, and you can gradually straighten the path taken by your skis until you go into the transition phase, and then follow it by starting the next turn.

These small fore-and-aft movements could make you think that you might get ahead of your skis in the first phase of the turn and be left behind them in the last. But if you take into account the way the skis accelerate in the first phase and slow down in the last, you can expect most skiers and their skis to stay together for most of the time.

initiating a turn, leaning forward correctly

SKIS

Although complex technologies are applied to the production of carving skis and they are shaped completely differently from classical Alpine skis, they are in fact a relatively simple tool for effective contact between skier and snow. *Their work in a turn involves the interaction of their two main features: waisting and flex.* ('Flex' is the way in which their centre part curves upward and downward longitudinally, to the degree governed by their stiffness; there is also 'torsional flex', a twisting motion like that created by a Chinese burn, but which is outside the scope of this book.) In the transition phase, skis have both parameters at zero: the skis are not edged, so they are not making use of their waisting, and lying flat on the snow they are not flexed.

In the turn initiation phase, edging the skis produces two effects: the edged ski starts making use of the arc-like properties of the waisting, and the action of our centre of gravity focused on the midbody of the skis makes them flex, tightening the curve that the skis would normally follow.

In the control phase, both effects are the most pronounced: the skis are not only deeply edged but also deeply flexed as a result of the increased centrifugal force acting on the skier at this point. In the turn completion phase, the reduction of this flex and the engagement of the rear, less waisted part of the skis leads to the gradual widening of the turn radius until the path straightens out in the transition phase, ready for the next turn.

on the edges and flexing the skis, turning with a radius shorter than specified for the ski

LEGS

One of the essential things to do on carving skis is to keep your legs apart. If you've been skiing for some years and you want to make the most of the possibilities offered by waisted skis, you will need to combat the ingrained technique of keeping your legs close together. For skiing on carving skis, your legs and skis should be more or less hip-width apart in the transition phase. During a turn, depending on how dynamic it is and how far your body is leaning over, the various parts of your legs will change their position relative to each other.

knees and skis well apart

When you're turning rapidly and so leaning over a long way, one foot can come close to the mid-thigh of the other leg, with the knee coming up under your chin and yet, even so, the distance between your feet may not increase.

Having your feet well separated offers two crucial advantages over keeping them close together in the way that so many experienced skiers have learned. First, your legs can work independently, responding to uneven ground, and so helping you to maintain your balance. Second, when leaning over you can more easily keep your weight off the inside ski and make a turn on the outside ski using the inside leg to support you slightly, but only for the amount required by the type of turn you're making and the conditions. Furthermore, if you make waisted skis run too closely together they will catch on one another, and when you're leaning well over in a sharp turn, the inside ski

legs apart, working independently on an uneven surface

legs well bent and body more upright

will get caught in the snow. *You need to ski with your legs slightly bent. Bent legs can act as a damper, allowing you to absorb the unevenness of the terrain. However, at the same time you need to explore the degree of bending with caution, as the physical strain on you increases signficantly the more you bend your legs.*

An upright, visibly extended stance reduces the strain on muscles and joints, especially the knee, and to a great extent shifts the load from them onto the main leg bones. *But skiing on your edges with minimum skidding exerts far more pressure on your joints, sinews and muscles than the classical technique would do.* Skiing on your edges leads to a greater risk of getting strains, and this probability will be increased if you bend low.

In the turn completion phase and during the transition into the next turn, you may do one of two things, depending on the technique you choose. *If it's down and up, you should bend your legs a little at the start of the transition, and then straighten them completely by pushing yourself upward a little; this means you take the weight off your skis as you shift your centre of gravity from one side to the other, and then as you initiate the next turn, you bend them a little again.*

going from one turn through transition into another in the down-and-up technique (above)

In the compensation technique you need to begin with legs less bent in the control phase, then deepen the bend in the turn completion phase, to straighten them to their full extent in the transition.

In the following turn you gradually extend your legs until they are maximally extended at the apex of the turn.

going from one turn through transition into another in the compensation technique (below)

KNEES AND HIPS

How do knees and hips work in a turn? Skiing is based on the movements of the legs and the interaction between the joints. The ankle's fore-and-aft range of movement is seriously restricted by the ski boot, and so it plays a relatively minor role – apart from, of course, enabling us to tip our skis onto their edges and back onto the flat again. However, the knee and hip joints are very active in a turn.

Bending our legs in the fore-and-aft axis is the basic movement that we make most frequently in daily life. But the situation is more complex when our body leans over, and leaning over is a crucial component of a turn. The distribution of forces in skiing means that we must lean our body over to apply maximum pressure to the edge of the outside ski; this way, we avoid skidding and carve our turn effectively.

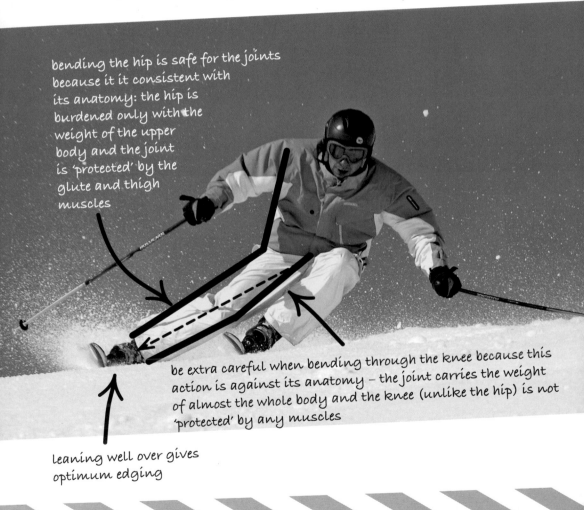

bending the hip is safe for the joints because it it consistent with its anatomy: the hip is burdened only with the weight of the upper body and the joint is 'protected' by the glute and thigh muscles

be extra careful when bending through the knee because this action is against its anatomy – the joint carries the weight of almost the whole body and the knee (unlike the hip) is not 'protected' by any muscles

leaning well over gives optimum edging

The sideways bend in our body is achieved through movement at the hip and to a lesser extent the knee. Whereas the anatomy of a hip permits a sideways bend, a similar movement, even though much smaller, in the knee is contrary to its anatomy. The hip is a ball joint and like a gear lever it allows both fore-and-aft movements and lateral movements; a knee, however, is a hinge joint and like a door can move freely in only one direction. Even a small degree of sideways bending will exert a considerable strain on the knee. So when bending the body sideways we should use the hips.

In the control phase, the body is leaned over to the maximum at the point when the greatest centrifugal force is acting on us towards the outside of the turn, and in order to counteract this and keep our balance, we need to achieve an effective edging technique, particularly on the outside ski.

the body leaning slightly, no sideways bend at hips and knees

hips slightly bent

hips well bent

In the turn completion phase, the lean is gradually reduced before disappearing completely in the transition phase, to be reintroduced on the other side when entering the next turn.

hips well bent, knees slightly bent

hips and knees bent

we twist
because we
lean, or ...

... we lean because we twist

UPPER BODY

A very important difference between the carving technique and the classical technique is the position of the body relative to the direction we're skiing in. In the classical technique, heavy emphasis was laid on keeping the upper body facing down the hill as much as possible, with the skis turning to and fro beneath. This led to constant twisting of the upper body relative to the direction of travel, and it was the strain and counterstrain produced in this way that allowed each turn to be initiated more easily.

But with carving skis we no longer need to carry out this unnatural manoeuvre because their very shape enables the turn to take place. It is enough merely to shift our weight from one side of the skis to the other, and as a result of this simple movement the skis follow the arc generated by their waisting. There is no need to assume a counterintuitive body stance that creates a conflict with the direction we want the skis to go in, in fact, quite the opposite, as our body can now actively support the movement. Our entire body points forward, in the direction we want to go in; the angle of the shoulders, hips and knees is kept as square as possible

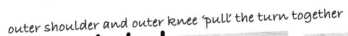

outer shoulder and outer knee 'pull' the turn together

the upper body stays still

hands and poles stay in the same position

relative to the skis. However, it doesn't matter if you find you tend to direct your upper body slightly downhill, but it is important that you don't let your hips twist so far that the uphill/outside ski moves forward, as you would in classical skiing.

So, to combat the habit of twisting the upper body in the downhill direction learned in the classical school, try to 'pull' a turn with your knee, hip and outside shoulder.

The upper body in a turn – in a long turn especially – is inactive and relatively immobile. We now know that the skis' waisting makes the turn take place, and it is merely by shifting our centre of gravity that we steer them and proceed from one turn into another.

ARMS AND POLES

Similarly, arms and poles remain almost still whilst carrying out a long turn.

In a shorter and more dynamic turn, our poles accentuate each turn by touching the snow lightly. This needs to be performed with a slight hand movement while the shoulder remains almost still.

In a short turn, especially in difficult conditions (on steep slopes and on moguls), poles and shoulders can start working more actively, and in a very short turn you can plant the pole into the snow so that it can be used as an axis to turn around.

pole planted in the snow

turning around the pole

In spite of the fact that the development of the carving technique has reduced the role of poles in skiing, they continue to be useful in difficult conditions, and also when queuing for ski lifts, climbing and on flat areas. There was a brief trend for no-pole skiing, but it seems that that's on the way out now; this is probably down to the realisation that poles can actually come in handy at any time, and they don't need to get in the way.

the pole touches the snow

skiing thro

...gh the air ...

COUNTERACTING MISTAKES AND BAD HABITS

The carving skiing technique is a natural way to ski. We stand on our skis in a comfortable position with our body facing the direction we want to go in, and make no unnatural or unnecessary movements. I re-emphasise that waisted skis will ski themselves, and we steer them mainly by shifting our centre of gravity. However, even in this elegant and natural way of moving, we still need to learn certain movements and positions.

A. DOMINANCE OF THE OUTSIDE SKI

One of the basic rules of turning in skiing is to put our weight onto one leg – the outside leg. *A simple law of physics tells us that putting our weight onto the edge of the outside ski makes that ski bite into the snow more deeply than if we spread our weight over both skis.* This depth of bite is particularly important on hard, steep slopes when only superlative edging allows us to control our line and protect ourselves from a sudden and unexpected skid, quite possibly ending in a fall.

Given that particular law of physics, *it's clear that we must always stick to the principle of dominance of the outside ski*: it's imperative to keep to this in difficult conditions, but it's also important when skiing in easier conditions, such as on gentler slopes and softer snow.

Skiing on one leg is to some extent contrary to our natural instinct to support our upright body on a wide base, resulting in a reflex to stand on both legs as much as possible. Counteracting this reflex is not that difficult, but does take some deliberate effort. The easiest way to achieve it is to practise an exaggerated version of outside ski dominance by deliberately skiing on just one leg.

skiing on one leg

To perform this exercise it's best to choose gentle blue runs with an even rate of descent, avoiding very flat sections – skiing slowly on one leg is likely to be more difficult than skiing at a moderate rate.

As you get more skilled, choose steeper slopes, and increase your speed and the time spent on one leg until this way of skiing becomes spontaneous. Remember, however, that while you're skiing normally, the inside leg should remain on the snow and play a more or less supportive role.

B. LEANING FORWARD

The second position in skiing that doesn't fully correlate with our inbuilt reflexes is the need to lean forward and apply pressure to the ski tips during the turn initiation phase. This stance has some essential advantages over the more instinctive backward lean (i.e. skiing on the tails) that can so often be seen on the slopes. First of all, by leaning forward a little we engage the front half of the skis in the turn, cutting the path along which the rest of the ski is to travel. Second, due to the deeper sidecut in the front part of the skis, we create a tighter arc, and by increasing or reducing the pressure on the tips we can modify the turn radius as we wish. Another significant advantage of skiing on the tips is the far lower risk of our skis slipping forward from beneath us than when we ski on the tails, which can so easily result in a sudden fall backwards – often surprisingly painful.

There are a number of exercises to help you learn to apply pressure to ski tips.

The first method is to deliberately lean forward during regular skiing, especially at the initiation of a turn. *The amount of pressure you will feel on your shins from pushing them against the tops of your boots will reflect the degree of your forward lean;* and if you're

putting pressure onto the tips of the skis by pressing down on the knees lucky enough to have someone to take photos of you – or, better to film you – you'll be able to observe the contact of the front part of the skis with the snow in all turn phases, providing the feedback to prove it beyond any doubt. If, like many people, you find it difficult to push your legs forward in this way, you can practise by skiing with your arms pressing your knees down, so that your shins are pushed down onto your boot tongues. Another exercise, which can be combined with the controlled arms exercise (see below), is skiing with the sticks held together in a horizontal position, which you push forward each time you start a turn.

C. CONTROLLING YOUR ARMS

Skiing is a dynamic exercise; shifting the centre of gravity from one side of the skis to the other alternately while balancing when leaning over as far as possible is rather like balancing on a tightrope. Just as a beginner tightrope walker will swing his or her arms wildly, when you're learning to ski you are going to make many movements with your arms and shoulders in the attempt to keep your balance. With time and practice, however, both the tightrope walker and the skier realise, as they develop their skill, that *the more economical the arm movements and the more controlled the arms, the easier it is to balance; that's why you should strive from the very beginning to control your arms, limiting their movements to a minimum*. When you're making a wide, gentle turn, your arms should remain almost still. Also, in the second and third phases of the turn, because of the bend being made by your hips (see photos below), your shoulders and arms should be as near-parallel to the ground as possible.

shoulders and arms held parallel to the ground

This is the ideal that you should strive to achieve. In reality, of course, you will see countless instances of skiers holding their arms in the wrong position during turns. The most common mistake is leaving one arm or the other behind; when bending downwards it is usually the inside arm behind, but when the body is over-rotated downhill the opposite happens and the outside arm is left behind. You will also see a lot of pole swinging on the slopes ... is this skiing or fencing, I sometimes wonder?

To stop your arms being overactive, you can bring them fully under control by 'freezing' them into a single correct and comfortable position.

poles held forward

To do this, ski with your poles together, held horizontally in front of you. As you get better at this, you can progress to keeping them apart in a horizontal position, but still at a balanced level.

D. BENDING SIDEWAYS AT THE HIP

The last element that can often be a source of difficulty when skiing the carving technique is the sideways bend at the hip when the body is leaning over in turns.

The natural response to increasing centrifugal force in a fast turn is to lean our body into the centre of the turn; this is what we all do when riding bicycles, and the same goes for speed skaters going around bends. But in skiing the base of our support does not follow the same natural projection of our centre of gravity as it would on a bike (where it's on the centre of a narrow tyre) or on skates. The base of support on skis is not the centre of the ski but its edge, which is positioned not directly under us but a

learning to push the hips sideways

short distance away. How far away depends on the width of the ski under the boot. So to apply maximum pressure onto that edge, we must shift our centre of gravity even further towards the centre of a turn, by pushing our hip in this direction.

At this point, if we're going to keep our balance the upper body must bend the other way, and finally we'll be on an edge with just the right amount of pressure, with maximum bite into the snow. The two effects combined provide the thing we need most in a dynamic turn – precise ski guidance.

The best way to learn how to bend your hips correctly is to deliberately thrust the inside hip sideways, towards the centre of a turn, during regular skiing. It is also helpful to get feedback via photos or films, or from friends you ski with so that you can check your progress.

If you find it very difficult to perform this sideways thrusting movement, maybe because of your normal posture, your body type or simply because you have stiff hips, you can help yourself by literally pushing your hips sideways with your outside hand (see photo on page 140).

E. OUR PERCEPTIONS V REALITY

Finally, it's worth bearing in mind at this point that our perceptions of our own movements can be inaccurate; we often feel that we're doing something that we're actually not. For example, on hearing the instruction 'Keep your arms forward,' we're likely to reply, 'But I am!' as we will feel that our hands are stretched out as far forward as possible, whereas in fact they're in line with the upper body or even held backward (again, photos and videos, if available, can show this up clearly). That's why you shouldn't be worried about making exaggerated movements when you're learning; if you want to change, say, the habit of leaving your arms behind, you will need to start by stretching them out into a position that feels unnaturally far forward. After a while you'll find that they're actually in a comfortable position – just where they should be.

THE FUN OF SKIING

Skiing is such a wonderful activity because it's a combination of communing with nature and seeing incredible views, undergoing a series of physical challenges, and basking in the euphoria that results from moving with speed and grace. In addition, although skiing is an individual sport, skiing in a group can increase the pleasure, as it enables you to give and receive helpful feedback while having fun both on and off the slopes.

As with similar activities that engage a combination of upper, lower body strength along with balance and coordination, the whole thing is about striking a balance between the respective demands.

That's why it's a good idea to do a thorough programme of pre-ski exercises before your holiday, to get real enjoyment from your skiing and minimise the risk of sore muscles and injuries.

As we have discussed, to enjoy skiing and ski confidently – whether quickly or slowly – and safely, you need to work on your skiing technique. We now know that the modern technique of carving is based to a large extent on natural and intuitive movements. But if you don't fix old habits and incorrect movements it becomes more and more difficult to eliminate them.

So you need to hone your technique to get more pleasure from skiing, for greater safety and to keep healthy. But you don't need to work on it like a fanatic: set yourself simple, specific goals, such as learning one or two essential elements of the technique or eliminating a single bad habit. For instance, while you can always hope to perform all the elements of a ski turn correctly, it's sensible in reality to focus on one specific element at a time, perhaps working on the dominance of the outside ski or controlling your arms.

And don't forget the wonderful views and the companionship. Beautiful pictures and memories of good times spent together are the best souvenirs of your skiing holidays.

and that's
the end ...

... or just the
beginning

APPENDIX: FACTS AND FICTION ABOUT SKIING INJURIES

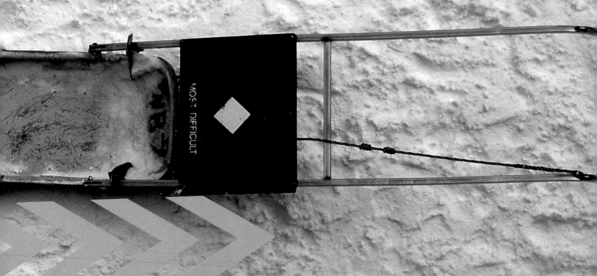

IS SKIING SAFE?

Over the last few years, winter sports have become highly popular. However, despite the fact that since the beginning of the 1990s more and more people have taken up snowboarding, skiboarding and cross-country skiing, nearly 70 per cent of everyone on the slopes is downhill skiing. When carving skis were introduced in the mid-1990s it boosted the popularity of skiing even more – beginners progress faster on them, and they enable advanced skiers to do tricks they could only dream of in the days of classical skis. It is estimated that there are now about 200 million skiers worldwide, and 70 million snowboarders.

Ski injury studies were first carried out at the beginning of the 1970s. Since then the number of injuries has almost doubled, but even so they are not as frequent as many people believe. Skiing has become safer because pistes are better prepared and marked, and a great many injuries have been prevented by better boots and bindings. Carving skis, too, have contributed to increased safety; they are easier to steer (especially helpful for beginners), so falls, and hence injuries, are less common.

On the other hand, ski slopes now attract snowboarders, who take different routes down the hill from those taken by skiers; this means more collisions occur at higher speeds. So the number of serious injuries, including complex fractures and head injuries, has increased.

On average, 2–4 injuries are sustained every 1,000=skier days. But the risk of injury to beginners is five times higher than to advanced skiers, mainly because beginners tend to go too fast on slopes that are too difficult for them.

Women tend to have knee injuries (especially injuries to the inner knee ligament, the medial collateral ligament). Men have fewer accidents than women do, but they have more serious ones, including head and neck injuries; this is probably due to more dynamic and faster skiing. Injuries sustained by children are most commonly fractures of the tibia.

The risk of injury is higher to people over the age of 26. On the face of it, this would seem to be an unlikely statistic, but it is most probably due to the fact that people in their mid-20s upwards tend to do less sport and be more deeply involved with their professional work. This means that they have less time for skiing trips (and, therefore, practice), but once they finally get onto the slopes they want to make the most of the time spent there. Add to this the fact that they have passed their lifetime peak of physical fitness and the tendency to believe that pre-ski exercises and warm-ups are a waste of their valuable spare time and it is not difficult to see why this is a high-risk age bracket.

COMMON INJURIES

Leg injuries account for 55 per cent of all ski injuries, and most of these (36 per cent of injuries) affect the knees. One in three ski injuries is to arms and hands – mostly the thumb (skier's thumb, which typically occurs when the thumb is wrenched backward from the hand, for example, when a skier falls on their outstretched arm while holding a ski pole) and the shoulder – dislocations, injuries to the acromioclavicular joint (the joint between the collar bone and top of the shoulder blade). Also, poor posture when skiing can lead to rotator cuff injuries (i.e. in tendons such as the superior spinatus, responsible for complex movements of the shoulder) and fractures. Snowboarders, in contrast, tend to suffer more often from wrist injuries.

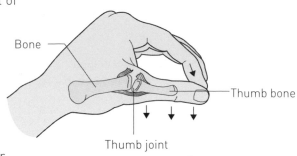

Bone

Thumb bone

Thumb joint

thumb ligament injury

IS IT WORTH WEARING A HELMET?

One skiing injury in five is to the head or spine. Many of these injuries are serious, involving concussion or even bleeding in the brain (intracranial haemorrhages). But the more serious injuries tend to happen to snowboarders rather than skiers.

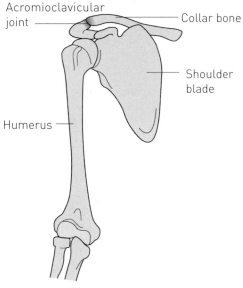

Acromioclavicular joint

Collar bone

Shoulder blade

Humerus

the shoulder joints

A number of injuries could be avoided by reducing the amount of people crowding the slopes, by creating safer pistes and by limiting the activities of the most foolhardy skiers. But helmets, despite appearances, don't solve the problem. They do reduce the number of skull injuries resulting from direct impact. However, brain injuries cannot be eliminated by helmets, as the data shows that skiers wearing them sustain head

injuries more often than those who don't; this probably results from a false sense of security and a willingness to ski faster and take higher risks. Therefore, helmets can bring about tangible benefits only if education about avoiding head injuries accompanies their use.

Skiers also experience other serious injuries, such as to the chest and stomach (mostly to the spleen and liver), but these are far less frequent.

THE TYPE OF SNOW MAKES A DIFFERENCE

If you fall on hard, icy snow, you are more likely to sustain an injury as a result of a direct impact to the shoulder, hip or knee. On this type of surface fractures happen more frequently, and head and backbone injuries are much more serious.

In powder, however, torsion injuries to the knee and ankle and spiral fractures of the lower leg, as a result of twisting, are more likely to be experienced.

DIFFERENT EQUIPMENT, DIFFERENT INJURIES

As skiing equipment has evolved, so too have the injuries. In the 1940s a broken ankle was the classic ski injury, because ski boots were very flexible, allowing plenty of mobility in that joint. Today's stiffer boots protect the foot and ankle, but, in doing so, the rotary forces have been transferred up to the knees, often causing injuries to the anterior cruciate ligament (a ligament found within the knee which helps prevent the thigh bone from sliding forward and backward on to the shin bone, see opposite).

THE KNEE IS OUR ACHILLES HEEL

Today, the most frequent injuries experienced by skiers are those to the knee, and the most common of these affect the medial collateral ligament (MCL) and the anterior cruciate ligament (ACL), ligaments that help to stabilise the knee joint. Almost one in two ACL patients will need to undergo surgical treatment; in addition, someone who has sustained an ACL injury and has not had effective treatment for it runs a six times higher risk of a repeat injury.

Skiing is the only sport in which ACL injuries occur as frequently in women as in men.

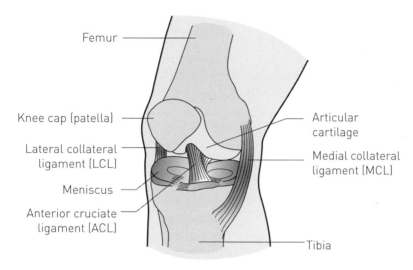

Femur

Knee cap (patella)

Lateral collateral ligament (LCL)

Meniscus

Anterior cruciate ligament (ACL)

Articular cartilage

Medial collateral ligament (MCL)

Tibia

structure of the knee

ANTERIOR CRUCIATE LIGAMENT (ACL)

The ACL is an essential part of the knee. It stabilises the joint and ensures its internal balance; it enables the menisci (see page 154) and cartilage to function correctly.

In most cases ACL injuries occur while falling with knees together (with the legs in an X-shaped position) and not releasing the skis. A popping noise can be typically heard at the time of injury, but many people can ski down the slope even after a rupture. However, an ACL rupture will hardly ever heal by itself; in most cases it remains damaged after injury, and the knee will never work properly without a fully functional ACL. Further injuries will follow – 80 per cent of ACL patients lose at least one meniscus

within two years of ACL rupture, adding to the increasing degeneration of the joint and cartilage, and the knee may become permanently useless within 10–15 years.

This is the reason why any ACL injury needs careful reconstruction. At present an arthroscopic technique is used to achieve this ('keyhole surgery', where treatment of the joint is undertaken through small incisions), and provided the patient then undergoes the full rehabilitation programme they can normally go back to their full range of sports activities within six months or so.

THE MENISCUS ACTS AS A SHOCK ABSORBER

Injuries to the ligaments go hand in hand with injuries to the menisci. The menisci are two semicircular structures composed of cartilage, the medial and the lateral meniscus, located between the tibia and the femur, and they play a unique role in the knee; they are the shock absorbers. Injury to a meniscus, such as a tear, leads to increased deterioration of the knee, and especially the cartilage in this part of the joint (with an injured meniscus, the pressure on the joint surfaces increases by over 300 per cent). As a result, after 10–15 years a knee injured in this way may need to be surgically replaced. That is why early diagnosis and treatment to save a ruptured meniscus (usually by stitching) plays such a vital role (see opposite).

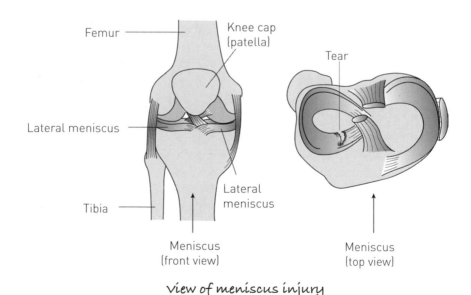

Femur —
Knee cap (patella)

Tear

Lateral meniscus —

Tibia —

Lateral meniscus

Meniscus (front view)

Meniscus (top view)

View of meniscus injury

Injuries to the menisci are mechanical, and because of that they must be repaired mechanically. In most cases this involves surgery. There's one very important thing to note. Many people think that if after some time they feel no pain, the problem has been solved; they believe that drugs, rehabilitation, irradiation, heat lamp treatment or physical therapy have worked effectively. But unfortunately this is not correct in most cases, because the menisci themselves do not sense pain, and so a reduction in symptoms does not necessarily mean recovery from the injury.

People who have injured their menisci suffer pain on the internal (medial) side of the joint or on the external (lateral) side, depending on whether it's the medial or lateral meniscus that has been injured. Sometimes it feels like the knee has given way, and has become slightly locked. There may also be some swelling or problems with straightening up or bending the knee. If so, a comprehensive diagnosis needs to be carried out, often including an X-ray. If medial meniscus injury is suspected, an ultrasound is normally sufficient for a positive diagnosis, but if the ultrasound appears normal and the symptoms do not subside, it is worth considering a magnetic resonance imaging (MRI) scan. Injury to the lateral meniscus, on the other hand, is so difficult to detect by ultrasound that, if it is suspected, it's best to perform an MRI scan straight away. In any case, always speak to a medical professional.

Anyone who has an injury to the meniscus will normally need to undergo surgical treatment such as stitching (suturing) in order for the rupture to be repaired. Removal of the meniscus is a last resort, and is now performed only when the meniscus has been very seriously injured. Collagen meniscal implants (CMI) can be used to help repair the damage as they provide a scaffold for the growth of new tissue in the meniscus, and menisci can also be transplanted from a donor.

FRACTURES HAPPEN, BUT PLASTER CASTS ARE PASSÉ

Almost half of all the fractures suffered in skiing involve a leg, usually the lower leg and knee. Many fractures, in particular those that are intraarticular (when the break crosses into the surface of a joint), require surgery. However, the good news is that today's fracture stabilisers usually allow the leg to be moved, so that rehabilitation can be started the day after surgery. So no more lying down with your leg in a plaster cast for months!

CARTILAGE INJURY

After a direct blow on the slopes, cartilage can be damaged or entirely torn off with a fragment of bone. However, some skiers have pre-existing cartilage problems that only become apparent when they're on the slopes, due to the increased stresses on their joints.

Cartilage injury is graded on a four-degree scale, from softened cartilage to a hole in the bone. Unfortunately, cartilage does not heal itself – any hole in it must be filled. It's best if the substance used for filling the hole is as similar to the natural joint cartilage as possible. This can best be achieved by transplanting cultured cartilage, which is done by taking some cartilage from the patient, growing it in a laboratory and transplanting it into the area of tissue loss. However, there are many other methods of repairing cartilage; an appropriate method is selected depending on where the injury occurs and how extensive it is.

WHAT SHOULD I DO IF I INJURE MY KNEE?

If after a fall you find any of these things:

- your knee is painful,
- your knee is locked (i.e. you can't straighten your leg fully),
- there is rapid swelling,
- you feel unsteady standing on the leg,

then:

- don't try to straighten your leg,
- put your leg into a position that hurts as little as possible, and try not to stand on it until you have seen a doctor,
- if possible, immobilise your knee in an orthopaedic brace or similar,
- cool the joint – swelling and pain will be considerably reduced (use cooling plasters or ice in a bag or frozen peas),
- get yourself taken off the slope, and see a doctor without delay.

In an injury clinic X-rays are normally taken in order to check for fractures, but an X-ray cannot show injuries to cartilage, menisci or ligaments. However, a clinical examination performed by an experienced doctor will normally be sufficient to make a diagnosis, which should help you to decide what to do next, even if all possible tests have not been carried out.

If you have had an injury, fracture or haemarthrosis (bleeding in the joint), if your leg is in plaster or if you're on crutches, always ask about blood thinners (anticoagulants) to help prevent deep vein thrombosis.

Deep vein thrombosis (DVT)

DVT is the formation of a blot clot (thrombus) in a deep vein, such as those found in the leg or pelvis. DVT is a medical emergency as the clot can dislodge and travel to the lungs, blocking the main artery. Factors that can increase a person's risk of DVT include immobilisation, such as a plaster cast on the leg, or lack of movement, such as when crutches are required. Blood thinners such as heparin are often prescribed to help prevent DVT.

Before you go skiing it's a good idea to take out insurance – it's not cheap, but it is well worth it! Having said that, what about also taking responsibility for your own welfare? Nobody can completely eliminate the risk of skiing injuries, but you can significantly reduce it. At least three weeks before going skiing, enrol on a course of pre-ski classes – many fitness clubs and rehabilitation centres provide them. Or follow the full course of exercises that you can do at home in chapter 1 of this book. Doing a course of pre-ski exercises will not only reduce your risk of injury, but can also improve the quality of your skiing holiday, as you will be less stiff and so be able to enjoy your skiing a lot more.

INDEX